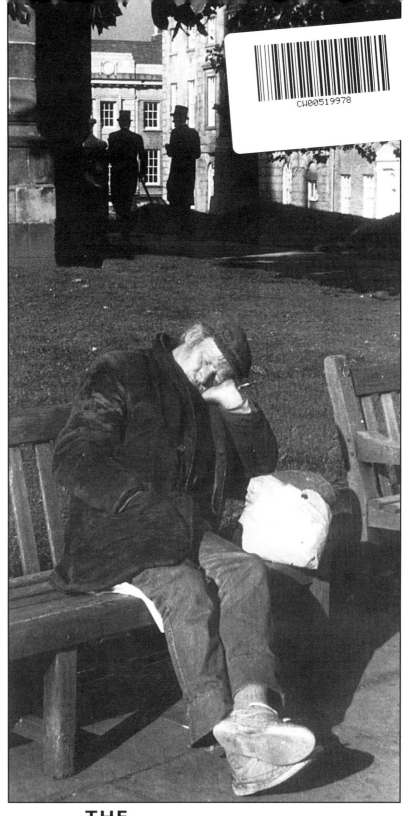

THE
SHEFFIELD
COLLECTION

Stephen McClarence

SHEAF PUBLISHING

Left: Whitehouse Lane, Kelvin

Below: Football Special at the Midland Station, early 1970s

Title page: *Installation of the Master Cutler, outside the Cathedral*

First published in 1992 by Sheaf Publishing Ltd, 35 Mooroaks Road, Sheffield S10 1BX
Copyright: Stephen McClarence 1992
ISBN 1 85048 013 3

Top: *Attercliffe Cemetery and Zion Chapel*
Above: *Franklin Street, Sharrow, 1966*

Birthdays are good times to take stock. And Sheffield's centenary as a city – its Charter was signed in 1893 – is a better time than most.

Sheffield in the early 1990s is a bewilderingly changing city. The old industries — steel, cutlery and engineering — stagger on, at a fraction of their former strength. The new industries — leisure, retail, sport — are taking over. In the process, as a new techno-wonderland is created, something is being lost . . . the character of the place.

Despite its Charter, Sheffield has always been more of a large town than a city. For centuries, it has been proud of its own working-classness, too busy earning a living to worry about its surroundings. Its centre has never had a truly civic feel, has never boasted more than a handful of impressive or distinguished buildings.

Quiet, sometimes accidental, corners of provincial charm have been its strongest card. Much of the city's housing — whether in terraced slums or the estates that replaced them — has been

depressingly bleak. Only the south western suburbs opening out into the Derbyshire Arcadia, have ever had pretensions to prettiness.

Its residents have been traditionally inward-looking, proudly provincial, preoccupied with their own parochialism. They know Sheffield is the best place in the world, but they want to keep it to themselves. They are 'not struck' with the imagined sophistication lurking beyond the city boundaries. It takes a Blitz to move them. They have shown a take-it-or-chuff-it bluntness and an indifference to (or inability to improve) their often grim surroundings. If there is mud, they will stick in it.

These qualities, though potentially negative and unconducive to change, are admirable in a truculent sort of way. They are now being eroded as Sheffield tries to come to terms with its own post-industrialism.

In the early 80s, after years of confidence, the city suddenly found itself in the wilderness of recession — a very literal wilderness in the East End, with its brick-strewn miles of industrial dereliction. Sheffield tried to re-invent itself. The World Student Games were staged and became part fiesta, part fiasco. Outsiders motored in with money-making schemes. These entrepreneurs, with their clean fingernails, may ensure the city's survival, but they are happy to leave it

Above: *War Memorial, Barkers Pool*
Left: *Figtree Lane from the Star offices*

looking as anonymous as any other town or city in Consumer Mall Britain. Often with the encouragement of a council panicked into grasping any lifeline, they demolish the very fabric that makes the city such a warm and characterful place and replace it with retail sheds just like the sheds in Loughborough or Leicester or Luton or any other station down the railway line to London. Sheffield seems hell-bent on abolishing its past, on breaking the continuity of centuries, on bulldozing the foundations of its greatness. Sheffielders are starting to feel outsiders in their own city.

So, one way or another, much of the city's heritage — a tradition of grit and grime that has nothing to do with the dinky 'heritage' hijacked by tourism — is disappearing. This book aims to capture some of it before it has gone forever. It's an admittedly partial — and partisan — record of a city that knew what it stood for, a city of industrial self-confidence and urban strength. It's a tribute, if you like, to the Sheffield preference for looking backwards rather than forwards, to a perverse nostalgia for gaslamps glowing through pea-souper fogs and furnaces erupting in the night.

Not that it started out so single-mindedly. I never intended to document the city in any systematic way. Most of the pictures here are street photographs taken out of curiosity in breaks from my work as a columnist on *The Star* — in pursuit of a hobby that has gradually developed into a parallel, if necessarily spare-time, career. Over the past ten years — mainly thanks to the encouragement of *Yorkshire Art Circus*, the West Yorkshire-

based people's historians — I have expanded my photography into exhibitions and book illustrations. I have been commissioned to photograph day-to-day life throughout Yorkshire, though strangely never in Sheffield itself. Only the pictures of the cutlery industry were taken for a specific project (an oral history).

My work at *The Star* involves a great deal of travelling around Sheffield — generally by bus (I don't own a car). I rarely take my camera with me on these jobs. Responding to an event in a way that makes a good article is very different from responding to it in a way that makes a good photograph. So most of these pictures were taken on days-off and at weekends, from the mid-1970s onwards. That they now seem to form premeditated groups is a tribute to the ability of Terry

Left: *Corporation Street*
Right: *Midland Station, 1984*
Below: *Broomhall, 1980*

Cooper of Sheaf Publishing to trace themes and connections. I never suspected I took so many pictures of doorways.

All photographs are to some extent about the camera that took them. Close-up studies of unsuspecting 'victims' making fools of themselves are made possible by telephoto lenses. A picture freezing a split-second of balletics at a football match may owe a great deal to motor-drive. The pictures in this book are a product of the most basic equipment — a Balda bellows camera which my father bought from the Co-op in 1953 for £10. It has recently been revalued at £8. He bought it primarily to document my childhood. It went with us on caravan holidays to the East Coast and the pictures of me, my mother and grandmother on the sand dunes at Anderby Creek are still there in the family album. As a child I borrowed the camera from time to time, though I can't remember whether I used it for my very first photographs — on a school trip to Stratford-upon-Avon when I was ten.

As I borrowed it more and more, I came to view as virtues what others would regard as inadequacies. No speed faster than one-two-hundred-and-fiftieth of a second. No aperture beyond ƒ22. No 35 mm flexibility — this was two-and-a

quarter square. I soon learned what the camera could do and what it couldn't do. If I wanted a close-up, I had to go in close. If I wanted a 'candid' close-up, I had to go in close and contrive to make myself invisible. Partly thanks to a suspicion of gadgets, I have never used flash (destroys atmosphere) or bothered with exposure meters or rangefinders. I estimate exposures by gazing meaningfully into the sky and, if the distance is crucial — in say, a badly lit room — I pace it out or use a tape measure. With portraits, this has the advantage of relaxing people. If a man with an ancient camera asks them to hold a tape measure to their nose, they assume he's a crank and stop worrying.

As a result of using this one camera for close-on 30 years, it has come to seem an extension of me. I take it to the repairers for regular patching up as a spring wears out or another pinprick hole appears in the worn bellows. But using this comparatively primitive Balda isn't a fogeyish affectation. The point is that it doesn't distract me from the pictures I want to take. Bags bulging with gadgets weigh you down and offer endless and often confusing photographic options. My camera, and the 400 ASA film I always use, don't. I think it was £10 of my father's money well spent.

Local Pubs

A Campaign for Real Pubs is inevitable. Breweries will be urged to stop ripping out real Victorian fittings and replacing them with fake Victorian ones. Then lovers of cigarette smoke, pub quizzes, ploughman's lunches and the curious ritual of the 'lady's glass' will be able to gaze at their empty dry-roast peanut packets and reminisce about sawdust and spittoons.

Right: *The New Inn, Ecclesall Road*
Below: *The Salutation Inn, Attercliffe, before demolition*

Top: The Rising Sun, Pear Street, Sharrow in 1973
Above: The Old Horns Inn, High Bradfield
Left: The Saddle Inn, West Street

Right: Randall Street, Highfields
Below: From the library at Upperthorpe

Writing on the Wall

The Hill Street Free Beer Store is now demolished, the Sarsaparilla (a long word for such a small wall space) Shop a newsagents and Upperthorpe Ales and Stouts full of padded bed heads. But the drinking goes on all the same.

Right: Attercliffe Road
Below: The Queen's Head, Attercliffe

Top: *Buddy Holly Convention at the Royal Victoria Hotel*
Above: *Flyposting in West Street*
Left: *Bus shelter on the Manor Estate*

Street Art

Revolution or oppression – a quaint reminder of Sheffield's radical days. Protest is now more likely to take the form of graffiti daubed on bus shelters or homelessness posters on Bacardi ads.

Left: Park Hill
Below: Frog Walk, Sharrow

Taking a Break

Ashelter from the rain, a place to enjoy an ice-cream, a chance to discuss modern art in all its outdoor modernity...Sheffield's art galleries have always been places to sit. And, with any luck, to think.

Left: *Lowfields*
Below: *Weston Park*

Above: *Outside the Mappin Art Gallery*
Left: *In the Graves Art Gallery*

Pastimes: I

The City of Steel has become the City of Sport. Athletes in pastel leisure wear and trainers are taking Sheffield urgently into the next century. On a less organised level, much sport goes on already. Spreadeagled climbers finger-inch their way up sheer walls. Council workmen tend bowling greens with curious rituals. At Swallownest, the National Whippet Racing Federation held its Fifth Annual Straight Championships. And Parkwood Springs — before the ski slope — regularly hosted motorcycle scrambles. Others enjoyed the quieter pleasures of dahlia-spotting in warm and stuffy marquees at the Sheffield Show, in its great days in the city's parks.

Left: *Parkwood Springs*
Below: *Wallclimber and jogger, Endcliffe Park*

Left: Whippet Championship at Swallownest
Below: Manor Community Centre

The Sheffield Collection

Pastimes: II

Left: *Burbage Valley, near Fox House*
Below: *Sheffield Show*
Right: *Fargate, early 1970s*
Bottom: *Langton's Snooker Hall, Heeley*

Right: Arthur Hales in his
shop, Greystones
Below right: Barber's
shop, Attercliffe Common

Above & right:
Saul's shop in Walkley

The Corner Shop

Saul's Noted Bacon Shop has long been a feature of Walkley shopping centre. At the far end of South Road, it was famed for its ham and its farmhouse cheeses (and noted for its bacon) for 58 years. It stayed in the Saul family until 1989, complete with shining red bacon slicer and hooks — and was then taken over by a customer who couldn't bear the thought of being deprived of Noted Bacon.

Shopping is now Britain's major leisure pursuit. Great cathedrals of consumerism are rising everywhere. But a few small shops still survive. The most fascinating of them are often corner shops, with their striped awnings and their shelves stacked high with Brasso and Paxo stuffing mix, dwarf dried peas and long-burning firelighters, piccalilli and carpet shampoo — everything you can't buy elsewhere. Like Arthur Hales' corner shop in Greystones, they are community centres, reassuring focal points for surrounding streets, part of the warm fabric of neighbourhood life. Their number has halved in Britain since 1972. Garages sell everything now, says Arthur, ruefully.

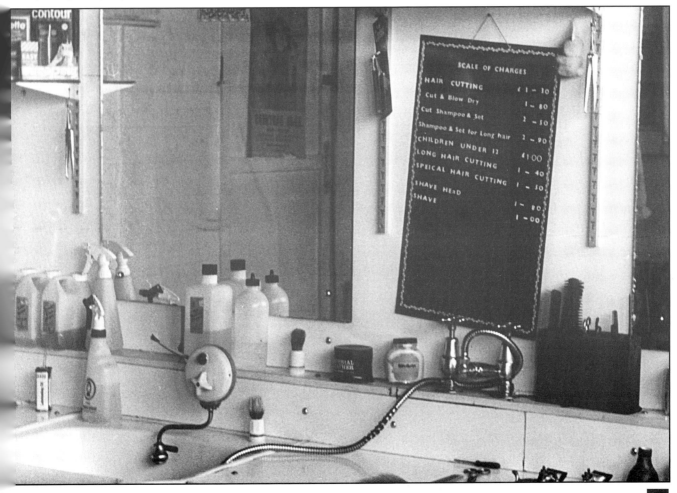

Window Dressing

Many shopkeepers employ window cleaners every morning. Their windows emerge bright and sparkling, reflecting light like mirrors. This makes life very difficult for photographers, whose reflections can often be glimpsed hovering ethereally. As in the Cooked Meats window.

Top Left: Jack's Sarsaparilla Bar, Infirmary Road
Above: Sharrow
Left: Broomhall
Right: Betty's Salon, Attercliffe Road

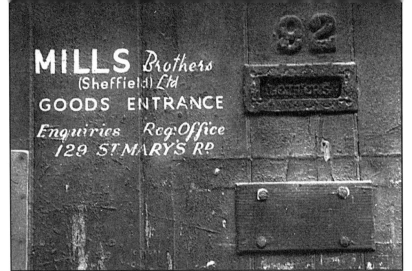

Frontages: I

Green Lane's triumphal archway is the grandest of entrances. Art and Industry united in its heroic carvings. But the more modest doorway of Morton's cutlery shop opened into a world of endless fascination — a world of Bead pastry forks, King salad servers, Rat-tail fish eaters and Harley grapefruit spoons. 'We have thousands of lads who just want to look at knives', said owner Hugh Morton, before he moved his shop further up West Street. 'They come in pairs and chatter like magpies.' Scissors are a speciality — twelve-inch paperhangers, five-inch nurses, ten-inch side bent, folding nail, curved manicure stainless.

Round the corner, Harrisons — slogan: 'Height for Hire' — is Sheffield's oldest steeplejacks. An early Harrison was the first man to climb Nelson's Column.

Right: Harrison's Steeplejacks in Regent Terrace
Far Right: Green Lane Works
Below right: Mortons old Cutlery Shop in West Street

Top: Doorway in Mary Street
Above: Passage at Stainton Road, Greystones
Right: Doors in Westfield Terrace

STEEPLEJACK
OF NELSON COLUMN FAME

Right: *Collinson's School of
Dancing in Hanover Square*

Frontages: II

Left: *Shop front in Infirmary Road*
Below: *Firth Brown's in Carlisle Street*

Archways

Long before traffic planners pushed people into underpasses, tunnels burrowed under Sheffield. Under the railway line at Cutlers Walk, under flats at Edward Street – and under people's bedrooms in a thousand terraces.

Left: *Edward Street flats*
Below: *Cutlers Walk, Heeley*

Above: *Railway bridge at Heeley Bottom*
Right: *Pedestrian underpass at Ecclesall Road*
Left: *Passage in Highfields*

Above: *Ted Butler in his Broomhall flat*
Right: *Stacked 'block' signs after demolition*

Broomhall

When they opened in the early 1970s, Broomhall Flats were hailed as a breakthrough in council housing. The mistakes of Kelvin and Hyde Park wouldn't be repeated, said the architects. This was architecture on a reassuringly human scale. The reality though, was a Lego-like labyrinth of dull concrete and bleak sunless tunnels. Many tenants were alienated by the place. They shut their front doors and felt hermetically sealed inside. The flats' structural failings led to their evacuation in 1986 and demolition in 1988. Few wept.

Right: Lift and staircase
Below: Galleries
Below Right: Refuse area

Far left: *Upperthorpe Library*
Left: *Saturday shopping*
Below: *Window cleaning in Westmoreland Street*
Bottom: *Kelvin galleries*

Kelvin

Government housing minister Ian Gow went walkabout in Kelvin Flats in 1985. He was taken to an empty flat and shown the bare floorboards, the peeling paintwork and the torn wallpaper. 'It's quite big, isn't it?' he beamed. 'And actually, you could make it super.' This has not been a common verdict on Kelvin, the great concrete fortress dwarfing the terraces of Upperthorpe, replacing their homely brick and slate with slab concrete, their decorative curves with Stalinist straight lines. Tenants have repeatedly complained about damp, cold, poor sound insulation, rotting concrete balustrades, insects, lack of play areas, and the problem of trying to sleep in bedrooms directly under the snaking walkways. Not too super. Demolition is planned.

Pensioners

Sheffield has more pensioners (and incidentally, more magpies) than any other British city. They are urged to campaign militantly by SPAG — the Sheffield Pensioners' Action Group — and mildly sent up by SPLAF — the Sheffield Pensioners' Liberation Army Faction, with its General Secretary, Betty Spital.

Top: *Pensioners in Darnall*
Above: *Checking change in Crookes*
Right: *Demonstrating against the Poll Tax in Snig Hill*
Far right: *Walking in the Botanical Gardens*

Above: *Rag and bone cart in West Street*
Right: *US Invicta in Wilkinson Street*

Vintage Vehicles

To a non-driver, cars have to be old to be attractive. Connoisseurs admire their imaginative use of curves — compare the boxy functionality of most modern cars. They stream across the city every morning and evening, taking people who live in A to work in B, and people who live in B to work in A. If the drivers swapped homes, the roads would be instantly traffic-free.

Right: *Morris Minor in West Street*
Below: *Ford Capri on Ball Street Bridge, Kelham Island*

Sheffield's Other Residents

Sheffield's open spaces are not playgrounds for people alone. Often unnoticed, animals and birds lurk enigmatically.

Left: Dog at the General Cemetery
Below: Cat and urn in the Botanical Gardens
Top right: Cat and balustrade in Hunter's Bar
Below right: Pigeons in Hanover Square, Broomhall

MVSIC THE PAVILION DRAMA

PARAMOUNT PLACE FOR SOCIAL RECREATION

پاوین سینما

وں کی نیماری اور اعلٰی تفریح کا واحد مرکز

Top: *Attercliffe Pavilion*
Above: *Sheffield Playhouse*
Right: *Heeley Palace*

Stage and Screen

The velvet curtains swish back, every fold caught in a cosy glow of orange light as a warm womb of darkness envelops you . . . a prelude to the full escapist reassurance of film-going in the days when cinemas were picture palaces. Sheffield once boasted 69 of them, from the 320-seat *High Green Picture Palace* to the 2,300-seat *Gaumont*. Originally called the *Regent*, it was indisputably the grandest of them — marble staircase, cut-glass candelabra, lounges with frescoes of moonlit Italian gardens, Georgian tearoom, 25-piece uniformed orchestra. Mucked about with over the years, closed in 1985 and demolished. Vandalism. The *Heeley Palace* (demolished 1981) was a more local affair, graciously curving round London Road, with Reginald Dixon as its one-time organist — as important to its Heeley community as the *Pavilion* (demolished 1982) was to Attercliffe. After bingo had been and gone, it became an Asian cinema. The *Playhouse*, small and homely on Townhead Street, was similarly reassuring — a modest theatre that admirably met Sheffield's needs.

Above: *Inside Attercliffe Pavilion*
Right: *The former Gaumont at Barkers Pool*

The End of the Morning Telegraph

The *Morning Telegraph* – Sheffield's morning paper under various names for 131 years – closed on February 8th, 1986. On the last working day, journalists wore black, a coffin was ceremonially carried into the debris of typewriters and old press releases, and candles were lit in beer cans.

Above: *Editor Peter Darling*
Left: *Coffin with candles*
Below: *Reporter David Holmes and the coffin*

The Old Industries

The Globe Works was not always as celebrated as it is today. Back in 1970, as both the Globe and Green Lane Works were listed by the Government, Alderman Jim Sterland, Chairman of Sheffield Town Planning Committee, observed: 'We don't consider these buildings to be of sufficient architectural interest to be listed. Our experts have advised us that they aren't worth keeping.' Time has proved the experts wrong and the Globe Works — one of Britain's oldest surviving factories — has been restored and returned to craftspeople of the fax age.

Above: Cutlery works in Heeley
Top right: Grinders in West Street
Middle right: Repairs sign in Milton Street
Below right: Former cutlery works in Devonshire Lane

Below: *Steel works in St Mary's Road*
Right: *Joiner in Arundel Street*
Bottom: *Globe Works – before refurbishment*

Above: *Beehive Works, Milton Street*
Right: *Wall, Kay & Sons, Cutlers, in Arundel Street*

Metal Bashing: I

In the late 1940s, some 30,000 people worked in the Sheffield cutlery industry. Today there are fewer than 3,000. Some are outworkers — 'Little Mesters' if you must, though the term has been debased into cosiness. Across the yard and up the stairs at Beehive Works, Edna Stone mirror polishes in an unheated workshop. Walter Trickett's, cutlers, moved from its Trippet Lane premises in 1989 and the building (listed outside but sadly not inside) was gutted for redevelopment. Individual skills still survive — at family businesses like Ron Birch's scissor hardening and boring shop or at enterprising new companies like Hugh Crawshaw's, workshops, cordless telephones and all.

Left: *Gillott's Pearl Works in Eyre Street*
Below: *Terry Smith, holloware finisher at Hugh Crawshaw & Co*

Above: *Roy Furniss buffing*
at Walter Trickett's
Right: *Knife blades at*
Walter Trickett's

Metal Bashing: II

Left: *Scissor blanks at Ron Birch's workshop in Arundel Street*
Below: *Edna Stone mirror polishing at Beehive Works*

Right: *Brian Lidster and Mark Franey casting*

Above: *Mark Franey dusting a mould with bellows*
Right: *Brass boy casting*

Metal Bashing: III

'When we knock on the Pearly Gates,' said Brian Lidster with sulphurous smoke billowing, 'they'll say: "You'd better come in. You've had your share of Hell".' He worked at The Brass Foundry, a now-demolished nineteenth-century building just off Carver Street. The business, set up by Henry Baker in 1897, had lately concentrated on decorative brassware, including original brass monkeys. But over the years, it had made tonsil cutters, handles for leg amputators, four-in-hand harness parts for the Duke of Edinburgh, fingerprint apparatus for Scotland Yard and non-sparking scissors for firework factories. The brass was cast at 1000 degrees centigrade. 'I once poured molten brass into my shoe,' said Brian. 'But it sounds worse than it was.'

Right: Brian Lidster inserting a crucible into a furnace
Below: Cyril Ali filing brass

Attercliffe

Away from the demolished terraces, the abandoned factories and the bright new sports stadia, the East End (or Nether Meadowhall) repays a stroll. Both the Cemetery, near the end of Worksop Road, and Tinsley Locks offer the tranquillity to contemplate earthly things.

Above: *Firth Brown's listed gateway*
Left: *Tinsley Locks*
Right: *Attercliffe Cemetery*
Below: *Factory at Carbrook*

Right: Hoarding at Canal Basin
Below: Tow path near Bacon Lane

Above: Bacon Lane Bridge
Right: Warehouse and boats

Canal Basin

The Canal Basin is a classic corner of Unknown Sheffield. Built in the nineteenth century as a terminus for the Sheffield and Tinsley Canal, it was once the city's commercial heart. The railways rapidly superseded the canal and the basin fell out of use. It was last used commercially in 1970. But behind the dilapidated warehouses and their cooing pigeons, the basin has become a boatyard for pleasurecraft owners. Unhurried repair work, grassy banks, a row of silver birch trees, fishermen, bird watchers, walkers and an overall calm. Grand schemes to redevelop it as a Yuppified leisure-cum-offices-cum-housing complex came and went in the late 1980s. The canal beyond was cut through open fields in 1819 and now has a unique atmosphere of silent stillness.

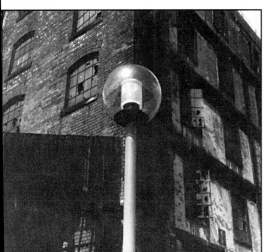

Top: *Sheaf Works at Blast Lane*
Above: *Warehouse at the Canal Basin*
Left: *The first signs of regeneration – dinky new lamps*

General Cemetery

The decline of the General Cemetery looks set to be halted. It was the last resting place of 77,000 Sheffielders — many of them young, some of them worthy, and one of them notorious. But, as with many Victorian cemeteries, disuse brought decay. The lower part was cleared by Sheffield Council in the late 1970s and early 1980s, and many fine and fascinating monuments — like that to figure skater Thomas Axe — were bulldozed. Small fragments of gravestones are still embedded in the paths. Words like 'Peace' and 'Beloved' stare up at you. Happily, despite the jungle of undergrowth, the top section, with the grandest monuments to the richest people, remains. It is likely to be conserved thanks to the enthusiastic campaigning of the Friends of the General Cemetery. Mayors and Master Cutlers are buried under every other angel — along with the notorious Samuel Holberry, the revolutionary Chartist whose 1842 funeral procession was lined by 50,000 people. Now deep in the bushes.

Above: The gravestone of Sheffield skater Thomas Axe
Right: The broken gravestone of Gizele Firth and her mother

Left: *The cemetery's Lion Gateway, mid-1970s*
Below: *Preserved gravestones with autumn bonfire*

Parks and Gardens

Sheffield is the greenest city in Britain, with the highest acreage of parks and woodland. And its strong tradition of allotments continues – a small plot of country for every urban working man (or woman) to rent.

Left: Rustlings Road allotments
Bottom left: Greenhouses at Rustlings Road
Below: Seats in the Botanical Gardens
Bottom: Allotments near Whiteley Woods

Left: *Swings and roundabouts at Sharrow*
Below: *Tethered dog in the Botanical Gardens*

Above: *Shadows in winter*
Top right: *Salvation Army rally*
Right: *Civic bonfire*

Endcliffe Park

Not quite the straggliest of Sheffield parks, Endcliffe — grandly graced by Queen Victoria — is perhaps the most versatile. It has hosted civic bonfires, horse trials and annual commemoration services for the Second World War American airmen who died when their plane crashed in the park.

Left: *Airmen's memorial*
Below: *Horse trials*

Above: *Grinding wheels*
Right: *Runner passing the Shepherd Wheel building*

Shepherd Wheel

Dark and damp and cold, the Shepherd Wheel — an eighteenth-century cutlery grinding shop last worked in 1930 — has not fallen victim to the heritage industry. It has not been turned into a cosy Disneyland vision of poor but picturesque working-class life with hands-on grinding opportunities. It's a reminder of the hardship of grinders' lives and, when the wheel is turning on Working Days, a glimpse of the importance of water power to Sheffield's early industries. Now verdantly nestling in Whiteley Woods, it's a familiar sight on the early stages of the Round Walk. Watch out for joggers.

Left: *The dam lake*
Below: *Interior with boots*

Still Life

The more inanimate and dismembered, the more potentially menacing. Second-hand shops offer many disquieting corners.

Above: House window in Brocco Bank
Left: Shop window in Endcliffe
Below: Abbeydale antique shop

Left: *The Library Theatre in the early 1970s*
Below: *Fallen angel at the General Cemetery*

Cobblestones

Cutler's Walk was a place to film *Room at the Top* or *Saturday Night and Sunday Morning* —a narrow cobbled ginnel between high brick walls. Northern industrialism at its grimmest. It led to a tunnel under the Sheffield-to-London railway line (the trains thundered alarmingly) and a path snaking along the River Sheaf. The cobbles are still there, but one of the walls has been knocked down and replaced by a fence separating the walk from a DIY superstore, whose bland piped music drifts surreally across. At the other end of the city, Attercliffe in the mid-1980s was still awaiting regeneration. Blaco Road, seen here from the corner of Belmoor Road, with Berkley Road first on the right, remained only as cobbles and kerbstones. And no piped music.

Top left: *Cutlers Walk, Heeley*
Above: *Guernsey Road, Heeley*
Left: *Blaco Road, Attercliffe before the East End redevelopment*
Right: *Daniel Hill, Walkley*

Down and Out

All these scenes of dereliction have themselves been swept away – many by becoming 'open spaces' with Astroturf grass and lollipop trees. The East End in particular, has come full circle and is as green now as it was before industry enveloped it.

Top: *Waiting for demolition in Highfields*
Left: *Derelict toilets, Highfields*
Below: *The former Carbrook Cabinet Company shop in Attercliffe*

Above: *Park Hill*
Left: *Attercliffe Common*

Evenings

These are all twilight pictures of Sheffield. But they could also be pictures of a new dawn. Let's hope.

Top: *Wards Brewery in Ecclesall Road*
Above: *Skyline at Hunter's Bar*
Right: *Lamp-post in West Street*